D1535353

RICHIE FARMER

with

Foreword by
Cawood Ledford

Antex Corporation
Lexington, Ky. 40503

An
Uncle Louie ®
Publication

Copyright © 1992 by Antex Corporation and Richie Farmer. All Rights Reserved. No portion of this book may be reproduced in any form, except for brief quotations in reviews, without written permission from the publisher.

Some photos appear courtesy of Chuck Perry, David Coyle, and Oscar Combs.

Printed in the United States of America.

ISBN 1-881079-03-1

Contributing Staff

Timothy L. Lester	Executive Editor
Susan Nelson Carey	Managing Editor
Stephen Kent	Chief Staff Assistant
Matt Clarke	Staff Assistant
Kitty Moore	Staff Assistant
Dennis Creech	Staff Assistant

This book is dedicated to my Granny Wolfe,
who wasn't here to share the joy.

Acknowledgments

I would like to thank my biggest fan. Mom, you've been there for every little thing. You're the organizer and keeper of the family and I can't thank you enough for being those things. You've supported me no matter what – you are the rock I turn to for love and guidance. I love you.

To Dad, thanks for all the long hours of hard work. You always provided me with everything I ever needed and most of what I ever wanted. You helped me learn how to dream, and gave me a love of sports I'll never outgrow. You have always been a wonderful example and taught me through actions, not just words. I love you too.

To Rhonda and Russ, I thank you for all the support and encouragement you've given me whenever I needed it. You are good friends as well as my brother and sister.

Finally, I would like to thank God for my wonderful family and the inner strength He's given me throughout my life. I know He has given me whatever opportunities have come my way.

Contents

Introduction

After spending many days with Richie Farmer, it is the opinion of this editor that in order for the reader to realize his multitude of accomplishments, I would have to be the one to tell about them. Richie is in no way self-absorbed. He finds it extremely uncomfortable to even mention all of the awards and titles that have been placed upon him. He is very humble about his accomplishments, almost as if they were commonplace.

I could not edit this book in good conscience without announcing all his athletic awards and records, so, here they are:

In 1984, as an eighth grader, Richie played varsity baseball and played basketball on three teams. He then played on the varsity team which went to the State Tournament quarterfinals where he scored two points. This was the first of five state tournaments in which he would play.

Then in 1985, he again went with his Clay County team to the State Tournament, this time to the championship game against Hopkinsville. He did better than his previous two points. Richie, now a freshman, scored 69 points in four games. Although the team fell short against Hopkinsville, 65-64, Richie's best was yet to come. This year he was leading scorer for Clay Co. with 16.8 ppg. He was runner-up Most Valuable Player (MVP) in the Kentucky State Tournament. He also achieved being a Kentucky High School Athletic Association (KHSAA) All State member, All 49th District, All 13th Region, All South Eastern Kentucky Conference (SEKC) member, and All Tournament member of the Ashland Invitational Tournament (AIT).

In 1986, his team was ranked number one in the pre-season polls. The team made it to the State again. The sophomore Richie scored 20 points in a losing effort against Pulaski County, 83-78. He was an honor roll student, school's leading scorer – 18.8 ppg, as well as All 49th District, All 13th Region, All SEKC, and an AIT All Tournament member.

Entering 1987 as a junior, Richie returned to the State Tournament with determination. He scored 27 points against Ballard, winning 76-73 in overtime. He had 89 points in four games. Richie was also chosen Most Valuable Player. He helped Clay County become the first mountain team to win the championship game in

31 years. He was the recipient of the Ted Sanford Award, chosen Player of the Year-SEKC, All 49th District, All 13th Region, All SEKC, Honor Roll Student, 1st Team All-State, All State in United Press International, and again the school's leading scorer with 23.8 ppg.

To finish his senior year in high school, 1988, Richie entered the State Tournament with tenacious courage to defend the team's title. Even though Ballard won, 88-79, Richie left his mark on the State Tournament for all to see. He scored 51 points in that final game, bringing his total points scored in five State Tournaments to 317. He was chosen Most Valuable Player for the tournament. Just in the State Tournament record books, Richie is in 12 categories:

> Most Game Points (51) he's second to Kelly Coleman.
> Most Tournament Points (137) second to Kelly Coleman.
> ** Tournament Points (317) topping Wallace Jones' 223
> Game Field Goals (20) – 4th
> One Half Field Goals (12) – 4th
> Single Tournament Field Goals (51) – 3rd
> ** Tournament Field Goals (127) over Wallace Jones' 86
> ** Game 3 point Field Goals (9)
> ** One Half 3 point Field Goals (6)
> ** Tournament 3 point Field Goals (15)
> Tournament Free Throws (43)
> ** Most Tournaments Played (5)

**Richie leads this category

Other than the individual records, Richie helped place his Clay County team among at least 10 categories for team records.

This impressive list only pertains to the State Tournament records. It does not include the honors he received throughout his senior year:

> Most Outstanding Player – Beach Ball Classic
> Most Outstanding Player – WYMT Mountain Classic
> MVP – Louisville Invitational Tournament
> MVP – Southeastern Kentucky Conference
> All 49th District
> All 13th Region
> All State – United Press International, Courier Journal, Lex. Herald Leader
> McDonalds All-American Derby Classic (Louisville)
> AAU Stars vs. Russian Nationals All Star Game (Lexington)

Dawahare's Academic Scholarship
Kentucky's Mr. Basketball
ESPN ranked him as one of top 3 small men in nation
Earl Cox picked Richie as the Most Valuable Player of the
     1980's Decade
Ranked #6 in class of 200 with a 3.6 GPA
Leading career scorer for Clay Co. High School – 2,937
     points
School record holder for most points scored in a single game
     (51)
School record for highest single season scoring average (27.1
     ppg)
During his 5 year career, Clay Co. compiled a won/lost
     record of 151-23.

This dazzling compilation of trophies somehow hasn't tarnished this young man from Manchester. He is polite, kind, considerate, and quite charming. Richie is also serious about any business he has on hand and is intelligent enough to handle it with ease.

I would like to say "Thank you" to Tom and Jessica for putting up with me and with our messy house while I worked to help finish this project. To Mom and Dad for help in stressful times. To the Farmer family who so graciously welcomed me into their home and made me feel a part of their family as well. To Richie for his friendship he's given so freely, I appreciate it.

Susan Nelson Carey
Managing Editor

Foreword

by Cawood Ledford

Richie Farmer is a Kentucky legend. He was a legend even before he came to the University of Kentucky and a bigger one after four years as a Wildcat.

He was the star for a Clay County High School team that captured the imagination of an entire basketball crazy state for four straight years. Richie rewrote the State Tournament record books and guided the Tigers to a state championship. His extraordinary talent on the basketball court made him a hero, not only to those in Clay County, but to all the people in Eastern Kentucky.

Despite an incredible high school career and being named "Mr. Basketball" at the end of his senior season, the University of Kentucky was not overwhelmed. Only after a barrage of phone calls to Eddie Sutton's radio program did Eddie finally relent and offer Richie a scholarship. The UK fans demanded that Richie be a Wildcat and his popularity grew during his four years at Kentucky to a stature rarely attained by a player. He is among the most popular players to ever wear the blue and white, and he leaves Kentucky as a star of the brightest magnitude.

Richie had to remind me of our first meeting. After he came to Kentucky, Richie told me of getting my autograph many years ago in his hometown of Manchester. We have since become fast friends. I admire him both as an athlete and as a genuine and caring person. For those who have admired him from afar, I hope through these pages you will get to know him better. If you do, you will grow to love and adore him even more.

While Richie's high school career is made up of the stuff we find only in fables, his career at UK was a far different story. During his freshman year (which was the worst UK season in memory), the NCAA was investigating the program and later stung UK with the most severe penalties in modern times. Richie, along with the other three seniors on the 1991-92 Wildcat team, were the heart and soul of the program that rose from the ashes to rank among the best teams in college basketball.

When I think of Richie Farmer as a Kentucky basketball player, I think of him as one of the great clutch players in UK's storied history. Richie was at his best when the game was on the line. Coach Rick Pitino never failed to have Richie in the lineup when Kentucky was clinging to a slim lead in the late stages of the game. If the other team had to foul, Richie was the player Pitino wanted at the free throw line. He never failed to come through.

As much as I enjoyed Richie as a player, I have come to enjoy him more as a person. He is class. The late Paul "Bear" Bryant used to say that he couldn't define class but he knew it when he saw it. I do too. And Richie embodies all that is good about college athletics. He is a very outgoing and giving person. He adores and respects his family. He is intelligent and caring and one of the most courageous basketball players I've had the privilege to watch.

On our pre-game call-in shows a question we got several times during each broadcast was, "Is Richie going to start?" If our answer was "No", the caller usually would plead Richie's case. If our answer was, "Yes", you could almost feel the pleasure and exhilaration coming from the other end of the telephone line.

Richie Farmer has had that effect on Kentucky basketball fans for the better part of his life. They perceive him as a star; a player who will come through when the chips are down.

How else can you perceive a legend?

When Richie called and asked if I would write the fore-word for his book I was highly honored. He is just one of the nicest young men you will ever meet. I just hope, through his words, you get to know him as I do.

1

Shots Through The Heart

I thought for a moment it didn't happen. I stood under the goal, my teammates around me, and for the first time in my life, I was shocked into unbelief. Christian Laettner's miracle shot just couldn't have been good. Yet, the fans in the Philadelphia Spectrum were going crazy, and the blank looks from my fellow players told me the impossible had really happened. Kentucky lost, just missing the Final Four, and my basketball career ended.

I believe I could actually feel my heart breaking. I couldn't really hear the words of comfort coming from Coach Pitino, my friends, or the fans. The assurances of a game well played were lost in the intensity of the moment. I simply didn't want to think. Thinking would come later.

It was great to play for the University of Kentucky, and I have enough good memories to last a lifetime. You can't believe the noise those people make when they fill Rupp Arena. I know; I've had them yelling for me a long time. Nothing compared to Senior Night.

I've been a part of the Kentucky basketball tradition all my life. I pretended to play for them, listened to every game on the radio, even stayed up late on school nights to catch the replays on television. Senior Night is the time when the coaches and the fans show their apprecia-

Busting out on Senior Night

tion and love for the effort a player gives during his time with the Big Blue.

Twenty-three thousand plus fans, wearing every imaginable combination of blue and white, and paying a king's ransom for tickets, crammed our huge arena. The lights went out. The band began to play "On, On, U. of K." Giant circles of paper with each player's likeness drawn on the front stood at the edge of the floor for each player to run through. My heart was beating so fast I was afraid I would trip or something else even more embarrassing.

The noise was deafening. Finally, I walked over to my mother and gave her a bouquet of roses. After the announcer introduced the four seniors, all the players and their families lined up on the floor and, along with the thousands of fans, sang "My Old Kentucky Home." I won't say if I was crying or not, but I finally realized I loved Kentucky more than I ever imagined, even as a boy

14

A Final Rupp Hug with Mom and Rhonda

in Clay County. That night, the long-time voice of Kentucky basketball, Mr. Cawood Ledford, retired, and I was selected to make a speech about him. Everyone, I suppose, thought they picked me because Cawood and I are both from Eastern Kentucky. They were partly right. Before each game, I walked over to the radio table and shook hands with Cawood just for luck. Senior Night, I was more nervous about the speech than I was about playing the game. After all, I didn't think there was much I could say about Cawood Ledford that hadn't already been said. Part of my speech stated, "As a kid growing up in Eastern Kentucky, Cawood was my hero. After spending four years with him, he's now my friend and still my hero." When it was over, I heard Cawood say the speech really touched him and made him teary-eyed. I was greatly honored to make the speech.

I can remember listening to Cawood call a game at the same time I was watching the game on television. He

A Tribute to Cawood Ledford

gave the game something extra. I don't believe the feeling will ever be the same without him.

He's done a lot for the whole game of basketball. I said, "I hate to see you retire, but I'm glad you're going out with us."

That event was the final time I would walk across the Rupp Arena floor as a basketball player. I know the past years of experience helped me walk out in front of so many people and face that microphone. It was the ending of a long and wonderful journey.

Richie and Cawood

2

Family Ties

I lived in Manchester all my life. It is a small town (population 1,634) nestled in the middle of the coal hills of Clay County, just southeast of Lexington. Interstate 75 and the Daniel Boone Parkway have made Manchester easier to find, but the town still hides among the surrounding mountains.

Some say it's low on night life, but I say it is high on beauty. Some may only see the dirt from the coal mines or the coal-stripped land, but if you look close enough, you can see the lush green grass and trees that color the rolling hills and the sky that is as blue as sapphire.

Clay County people are strong and full of life. Their hearts warm fast, and they're very friendly. Almost everyone knows everyone else. You can drive around and just about anyone you see, you know all about them. I mean anyone! In a way it makes you feel safe. You know you're not alone.

My parents, Richard and Virginia, older sister Rhonda and younger brother Russ all live in Manchester today. Mom and Dad moved to town from Big Creek, Kentucky. Dad drove a truck until I was six. In 1975, he became the transportation manager for a coal company. He was in charge of all the trucks and trains hauling coal, as well as checking the quality of coal for each customer. In 1991, after sixteen years with the coal company, Dad went to work for Metropolitan Life Insurance.

My mom worked at keeping our house together, and making sure Russ, Rhonda and I behaved ourselves. She also ran a clothing store named The Factory Outlet in downtown Manchester. She is a great mother, cook, and friend. She is also my biggest fan.

Growing up in Clay County is something I would never want to change. I've played ball with guys across the country. Some were from New York, Los Angeles, and Miami. Really, they came from all over the place. Still, every time I would hear them tell stories about their hometowns, I never wished to live anywhere but my own house in Manchester. One of the main reasons I feel this way is my family. They are great!

One time the three of us kids were in the living room wrestling and knocked the coffee table into the hearth. The table broke a piece of the hearth off, and knowing Mom would be upset, we vowed not to tell on each other.

Russ decided to get rid of the evidence by throwing the broken piece over the hill near our house. After a while, my mother came into the living room and saw the table moved and the hearth broken.

She turned right to me and asked, "Richie, what happened to this place? There's a piece broken off my hearth." I was sitting beside Russ and Rhonda on our couch afraid to move a muscle.

Then she said, "All right you kids, I won't get upset or whip you or anything if you just give me that piece so I can glue it back on."

"Rhonda," she asked, "Where is it?"

My sister answered, "I don't know, Momma."

Finally, she turned to Russ. He was the youngest and not handling the pressure of our silence very well, and Momma knew it. "Russ, do you know where that piece to the hearth is?"

Russ innocently replied, "I don't know Momma, but I think somebody probably went and threw it over the hill."

Mom couldn't keep from laughing, but even after we all went to look, we never found the broken piece. Today, that old hearth has a few more scars to prove kids will be kids.

My brother and sister and I had a great time in Manchester when we were kids. Like everyone else, we played a lot and fought a little.

Rhonda, at Four and Richie at Six Months

Anytime Rhonda wanted to go somewhere special, she had to ask Dad. I would hurry over beside him and say, "Don't let her go, Daddy, don't let her go. All she wants to do is drive around and chase after boys." Dad would ask her several questions concerning her outing, and if his answer looked promising for Rhonda, I always threw in, "If you do let her go, Daddy, I better go with her." Well, you can imagine she was always trying to get rid of me, and she usually succeeded.

When Rhonda and I were kids we would wrestle around on the floor, and chase each other all over the yard screaming and hollering. I think we just fought over who was going to be in charge. Thank goodness we grew out of this! Looking back on it, Rhonda and I were a great deal alike.

Richie, Rhonda, and Russ

Now that we're adults, we have a very close relationship. We talk on the phone just about every day, and we try to be as supportive as distance allows us to be. I confide my thoughts and secrets in Rhonda. She gives me sisterly advice about any problems I may have. Somehow, we are close enough to communicate without words. I guess that's what I love about her. She knows the real me.

Because of our close ties, I am becoming good friends with her new husband, Jamie Gray. We've known one another for five years, and we are developing a relationship that seems more like brothers than just brothers-in-law. We like to go fishing whenever we have the chance, and I take the pleasure of telling him stories about Rhonda growing up.

I also fought quite a bit with my brother. Most brothers do. We would fight to kill each other at the house, but when we got around town and somebody wanted to fight one of us, they'd have to fight us both. Many times Rhonda was in on the fight, too.

Richie and Russ

When Russ and I were little, about four or five, we would play in our granddad's barn. One day an old mule was loose and blocking our path through the barn. Not knowing it wouldn't hurt us, we decided to throw rocks at it to make it move. Russ stood just to the left and a bit in front of me as we began to throw. I found a good-sized rock, and as I released it, Russ stood up. I missed the mule but caught Russ right in the forehead. It split his head open, and he started bleeding all over his face and shirt. I was so scared. Thinking I had killed him, I rushed Russ up to our house and helped Mom with cleaning him up. She assured me Russ would live. He did, but he still has a scar from that adventure.

My mom has several more stories about me when I was a kid.

"When Richie was really little, anytime he cut himself and it bled, he'd come running in yelling, 'Mommy, put a band-aid on it before all my air gets out.' He thought he was going to deflate. I always kept a full supply of bandages in the house for his reassurance."

"I guess it was about age five that Richie started picking on people. When my three children sat on the couch to watch television, Richie would lean over and just touch Russ with one finger. Russ would yell, 'Mom, he's touching me!' I would tell Rich to stop, and then he would keep his finger about a hair away from Russ's skin just to irritate him. He loved to pick on everybody and still does."

"Occasionally, I had to discipline Richie. After I spanked him, he would look at me and say, 'When I get big like you and you get little like me, I'll spank you, too.' "

"Like all children, Richie was always getting into some kind of mischief. One day I was at a junk store and he ran off. In the back of the store was a place to have your picture taken. He climbed up and had his made without even telling me. We went home, but he never mentioned it to me. I guess it was a year later when a lady from Clay

County was in that same store. They asked her if she knew who the child in the picture was. She recognized Richie, brought it home, and gave it to me. I've treasured that cute keepsake to remind me of his childish mischief."

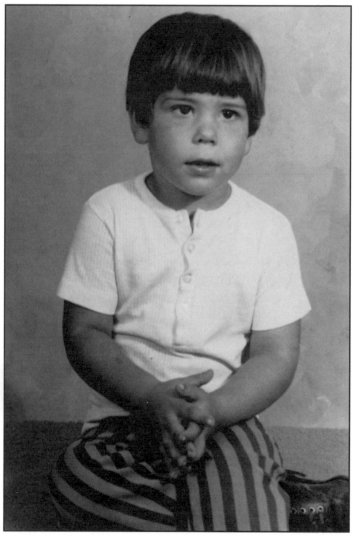

Famous Junk Store Photo

3

Building A Dream

It was my dad who introduced me to sports. He played basketball all his life, and when he was in high school, his team went to the state tournament of 1963. He received a full scholarship to play for Cumberland College, and that same year married my mother. He had a solid background in both baseball and basketball, and loved to teach both Russ and me.

I started basketball when I was about four. There was a basketball goal and a dirt court behind our house. Every morning I would eat breakfast with Dad, and as soon as he left for work, I started playing ball. Dad would show me a new drill to work on each day before he left, and that's what I tried to concentrate on.

Mom would fix bologna sandwiches and cold pops to drink so I could play all day long. I stayed on that hillside court from daylight till dark, and I never remember getting bored. Making up different games was part of the fun, and I invented something new each day. Horse, one-on-one, put-out, many games I could play by myself, and some with my brother. Mostly though, I just enjoyed shooting those baskets.

One of my early sports heroes was Kyle Macy; every now and then, I would pretend to be him. I set up game situations with UK playing Louisville or Tennessee.

25

With the score tied and time running out, I would bounce the ball off the goal post, dribble once as if an invisible teammate passed me the ball, and launch a thirty-footer at the buzzer. I never missed that shot!

Homecourt Advantage

If I got tired of being a guard, I put up another type of goal only eight feet high. I called it my "dunking goal." I used a smaller ball, changed roles, became Rick Robey or some other big center, and began dunking like crazy.

By the time I went to kindergarten, I told everybody I would play for the University of Kentucky. I don't think I ever wanted to do anything else. When I entered first grade, the teacher passed around a piece of paper on which we were to write what we wanted to be when we grew up. I wrote, "a UK basketball player."

Playing for the Wildcats is more than just a boy's dream. Where I was raised, if you are good enough to

26

make the team at UK, people never forget you. For me, to play anywhere but Kentucky would have been settling for second best. I knew if I wanted to be the best, I just had to go to Lexington. That perception may not be fair, but that's the way I felt about it. I was determined to be a Wildcat.

The first organized basketball team I played on was in first grade. My teacher at Hacker Elementary was Freddie Abner, and she bought us boys some tee shirts with numbers. She even coached us as we played the other first, second, and third grade teams. We beat them all. Mrs. Abner said, "I've taught school for 33 years, and they were the only first grade team that played ball the right way. They all dribbled the ball, they didn't walk, they used one hand, they would take it down the floor and pass before they would shoot. All of the boys were good, but Richie was the only one determined to really do it well."

That first grade team gave me a taste for competition and discipline I still can't get out of my mouth. It helped motivate me to practice longer hours and develop a 'touch' for the ball. By the time I was in second grade, we would play ballgames during physical education class. Our teacher, Mr. Les Carnahan, let us play other teams in the fourth, fifth, and sixth grade. Sometimes, he would arrange it with our teachers to let us get out of class and come play every once in a long while. I decided that was too long to wait, so I started telling our regular class teacher that Mr. Carnahan had asked us to come to the gym during classes. I was only in second grade and forgot that being out of class all day for several days in a row would get him suspicious. Well, Mr. Carnahan noticed that we seemed to be in the gym playing ball an awful lot, and once the truth got out, he lined us all up and gave us each one lick with a paddle. Believe me, after that I adjusted to only playing when I was told!

Minor League Baseball Team (Richie with Bat)

My dad not only taught me about basketball but about baseball as well.

"While Richie was trying out for the Pee Wee League at age five, the park manager was pitching underhanded to him. Richie hit a line drive back to him that just missed his head. The manager said, 'We need to move this kid up to the Minor League.' He started playing Little League when he was eight years old," said Richard.

"Every year he played Little League, someone would go to the health department to check his birth certificate. People simply found it hard to believe he was so good so young. Virginia threatened to post a birth certificate up at the ballpark each year, but Richie wouldn't let her. Many times parents would sit right behind us and say things about him so we could hear. 'I know he's a lot older than what they're saying,' or 'They've got fake birth certificates.' Virginia cried many a game."

"I guess he and his brother still hold all the records for homeruns, runs batted in, and a few others. I have always been proud of his athletic skills."

"By the time Richie was in seventh grade, he started on the varsity baseball team. He didn't just start, he led in many categories. Richie played up to his senior year, and then concentrated solely on basketball. I think he had the potential to play major league baseball. He was that good. I believe it was his best sport."

Johnny Hyde, Richie's sixth grade teacher, recalls, "Even when he was in grade school, he'd gotten famous. I remember once we went over to Hazard in a tournament, and there was a guy that came up and said, 'I want to see Richie Farmer, I've heard so much about him.' Everywhere he went, everybody knew him. He didn't think too much about it. He never got excited about it; he just took it in stride. He was mentally mature for his age."

"To many of the kids I teach, Richie's their hero. He gave our county something positive to hold on to. People may have only met him one time, but they feel as if they know him. Richie will make you feel that way, too. He's a good guy. He always seems interested in your life and what you have to say."

"From a father's standpoint," Mr. Farmer says, "I was amazed at his motivation from the very beginning."

"I could show Richie any kind of drill, and he would work on it all day. I guess that's one of the reasons he competed so well. He really concentrated on the game. It was the same in baseball. He insisted on doing his absolute best no matter what sport it was."

"I think Richie gets his competitive spirit from me. I always taught him that it was good to win, and he became very disciplined. I don't think that was forced on him; he chose to be that way. He always looked at things as a challenge. Then, he would tackle whatever it was until he mastered it. He rarely gave up on anything."

I always tell people one of the reasons I shoot so well

is because of where our basketball court is. It's up on a hill; if you hit the rim, the ball shoots way down the hill, and you have to go after it. That's pretty good motivation for getting the ball in the basket.

In the winter, I would spend hours shoveling the snow off the dirt court up on the hill. I would shovel and sweep and walk over the snow to get it packed down. The ball would barely bounce, so I'd bounce it until snow compacted all around it. Then the next obstacle to overcome was the net. It was so frozen the ball wouldn't go through. I kept a long pole to pop the ball back up and out of the rim. I would play until I was frozen solid.

I think the desire to play ball was in the mountain air because my dog, Beau, loved to play right along with me. He would run after the rebounds and help referee the close games. He barked whenever I would make a basket, or slept if I wasn't impressive enough. We always had a good time up on that dirt court no matter what happened. Beau knows basketball!

Beau Knows Basketball!

30

4

Hook-Shot

I would have gone crazy if the only thing I had done was play basketball. Growing up in Manchester gave me the opportunity to learn other sports like hunting and fishing. I enjoyed going out to hunt squirrels with my friends. One time, my brother, Ben Carnahan, Jamie Hollin and I decided to go squirrel hunting. Now, Ben and

Russ, Jamie, Ben, and Richie Taking a Break

31

Russ didn't really care much about hunting, but Jamie and I were more serious hunters. We went up the hill behind our house, and while Jamie and I were easing along, Ben and Russ were just tromping, breaking every twig and limb. At the top of the hill, I said, "We need to split up. Russ, you and Ben are making way too much noise." So Jamie and I went one way, and Russ and Ben went the other. After we got around there, I heard Russ and Ben start shooting. They must have unloaded their guns. We ran to where they were. "What are you shooting at? Did you find a nest of squirrels?" I asked. It turned out they were shooting a hornet's nest. I got madder than fire over that. That was the last time I would go hunting with Russ!

My dad took me hunting when I killed my first deer.

"It was his junior year in high school, and Richie had been out all day without seeing one deer. It started getting dark, so he headed back to camp. As he walked to the campsite, he spotted one out in the distance. He killed it right before dark," Richard Farmer says with a smile. "His determination paid off."

After the Hunt

"Whether he was hunting or fishing, whatever he caught, he'd want to mount it. When he was ten years old, Richie caught a seven and a half pound largemouth bass. He went to get a cooler, put the fish in it, and took it home. He was so excited. He showed it to Virginia and couldn't control his excitement. Richie really wanted to mount that fish. After he had shown it around the neighborhood, he asked Virginia if he could get it mounted. She said he had to call me at work."

" 'Dad, I just caught this seven and a half pound largemouth bass. Can I get it mounted?' He asked anxiously."

"Do you have the $77.00 it will take to mount it?"

" 'No.' Richie said in return."

"Then put it back, I said. He has never let me forget that was the largest largemouth bass he ever caught."

"Richie was an excellent shot," testifies close hunting friend Beve House. "He was a natural at it."

"We were driving down the road one day," said Beve, "and Richie saw a crow sitting in a tree over on a hillside across the railroad tracks. It was about 250 yards away. Richie told me to stop the truck, and stated that he was going to shoot that crow in the head."

"I said, 'No, I don't want you to waste my shells!' Richie was determined, so he aimed his .308 rifle at the crow and fired. I just laughed because I thought he couldn't hit a bull that far away. As soon as he fired the crow fell out of the tree. I couldn't believe it! He'd hit that bird in the back of the head."

"Another time, Richie and I were riding around scouting for ponds to frog hunt in. We had a spotlight in the car and began shining it out the car window from up on the highway. We knew there was a pond around there somewhere. We didn't know, however, that a state policeman was there as well. A blue light came on behind us, and we pulled over. The policeman walked up to the passenger's door. Richie rolled the window down; the policeman asked, 'What are you two doing?' "

"Richie quickly said, 'We're frog hunting, officer.' "

"Puzzled, the patrolman laughingly responded, 'You sure are going to catch a lot of frogs up here on the highway.' "

"I think he was too confused to give us a ticket," Beve said.

Another hunting buddy was Russell Wolfe.

"Once Richie and I went frog hunting. Richie took his Springfield .22 single shot rifle. We were standing up on a deadlift when we spotted a pair of eyes shining in front of our flashlight about 40 feet away. Richie said, 'I'm going to shoot that frog.' "

" 'Richie,' I said, 'you can't shoot that frog from here. It's too far away, and you can't tell how big that frog is.' "

"It was an unreasonable distance to even think about shooting. He shot anyway, and the frog eyes closed. I had promised to retrieve it if he hit it. I climbed through brush and rock 'til I found it. Sure enough, he'd shot a frog that was about two inches long clean through."

"It didn't matter what Richie did, he was going to do it with perfection. He believed he could do it."

This belief applied not only to hunting but to basketball as well. When Richie was in the eighth grade, he had already played on the grade school (6th - 8th grade) basketball team since fourth grade. In seventh grade he started on the Freshman (9th grade) basketball team, as well as the Junior Varsity (10th & 11th grade) basketball team. It was the February of his eighth grade year when he started playing on the Varsity basketball team.

5

Sweet Victory – Bitter Loss

The Clay County basketball program has been a success for many years. My senior year, we were ranked as high as fourth in the nation. I'm sure Coach Bobby Keith is the main reason the team has had such success.

Coach Keith came to Clay County as an assistant in 1963 and became head coach in 1970. He seldom started freshmen on the Varsity team. He usually only played six or seven guys all the time. Many times his entire starting team graduated. Then he would use the underclassmen who had been playing those seniors in practice. Coach always, I mean always, got the best out of every player's ability. I think that's why he had a good team each year, even when the starting five left.

He taught about setting and attaining goals, both on the court and in my life. I learned about dedication and sacrifice, and most of all, believing in myself. Coach Keith is a very intelligent man, and I consider myself very fortunate to have had him coach me for five years.

Coach Keith's incredible memory always amazed me. He would come out for a game without notes or scouting reports, and begin to tell us what to watch for with each opposing player. He knew the player's name, number, how well he was shooting, and any other information we might need to know. When he finished, we knew exactly

35

Richie With Coach Keith

what our man could do before he did it.

Coach Keith also taught me something about responsibility. He has a very strong work ethic. He works hard every game. I think that's why he is successful: because he works harder than any coach in the business. Everyone in Manchester, Clay County, and the whole region loves him. He made our team feel we were part of something special. Now that I think back on it, Coach Keith was part of my family, part of all our families.

The year I started playing on the Varsity team, we went to the state tournament, where I scored my first tournament basket. It only counted two points, but for an eighth grader they were very big.

Some people ask me if I got tired, or if I quit playing ball during my summer vacations. They look a bit disbelieving when I tell them about our summer leagues. I was addicted to the sport. I played in all the summer games I could.

First State Tournament Basket –
Number One of Many

One of our summer teams went to the State Amateur Athletic Union Tournament (AAU) in Frankfort right after my eighth grade year. To win the tournament, a team had to win eight games in five days. As a member of the team from the summer league, I played against high school juniors and seniors around Kentucky. We won the AAU tournament championship and went to Brownsburg, Indiana, where we faced a Michigan team led by 6'11" Terry Mills.

The Michigan team was made up of the best fifteen basketball players in the state. Since we won the AAU championship, we could have picked up some of the other players around Kentucky, but we didn't. We wanted to represent Clay County and Manchester.

Now, I'm not going to tell you I wasn't intimidated when Coach announced I was to guard Terry Mills. Actually, with a minute left in the half, I walked over to Coach Keith and told him I didn't think I was ready to play at this level.

He took me out, but not without some words of wisdom. Coach Keith said, "Richie, I think you can play against anyone. I never want to hear you say that there is an individual you don't think you can play against."

He started me again the second half. My shooting

37

stunk in the first half, 0 for 10 won't get the job done anywhere, but I went 11 for 11 in the second half. We lost that game 90-89, but I ended up with 26 points, and Coach said he never worried about me competing with anybody again.

By the time I reached my sophomore year in high school, I had earned the nickname "grand master." The public address announcer, Stanley Abner, pinned that name on me. He said it fit me because of the way I took charge on the court. I played point guard, and my role was to help my teammates follow the coach's instructions. For whatever reason, the name stuck.

That year our team went to the state tournament, and Pulaski County closed the "grand master's" concert in the first round.

The "Grand Master"

After every close game, people want to know how it feels to be under pressure in those kinds of important games. I always say I guess I was used to it. During my high school career, the team, the coach, the fans, even the opposing team, all looked to me to take the shot at the end of every quarter or game. It came to be expected. Everyone in the gym just knew I would get the ball and take the last shot. I knew I could make them. I know there were times when the ball bounced off the rim, but I still would rather be the one shooting.

In 1987, we came back and won the state championship. I will never forget our final game: Clay County versus Louisville Ballard, loaded with talent, and led by Allan Houston. The game went into overtime when Ballard got a tip-in at the buzzer.

We had the ball with about 1:04 left in overtime. We were down by one point. This was my fourth game in four days; I was dragging up and down the court, so I signaled Coach Keith, who called a timeout just to let me rest.

Not many coaches want to waste their last timeout with so few seconds left. The game started again, and I felt much stronger. We had talked during the timeout about what we wanted to do. We were trying to relax, take some time off the clock, and get someone a good shot. It didn't matter when we took the shot, only that it was a good one. After the other players broke the huddle, Coach Keith held me back and said, **"I want you to take the last shot when the clock gets inside 30 seconds."** I looked at him and said, "I'll make it."

There's not much you can do in those last few seconds, but we were trying to run a pattern to free someone. Time was running out, and finally one of our guys got open. He spun around to shoot, stopped and kicked the ball outside to me. Two Ballard players were immediately in my face.

Now, few players want the ball in a game situation like this one. After all, who wants to be blamed for losing any tournament, much less the state championship! But I had years of imagining out back at our house, and I never missed at home.

The clock read 32 seconds. I looked at Coach Keith and nodded. I moved off to the right of the key, and spun back around to the left, right into another double team. I stopped and jumped as high as I could and arched a shot over both Ballard players. Swish!! It was Clay County by one. Ballard failed to score on their next possession, and after we made two last second free throws, we won by three points, 76-73.

State Champs at Last

The night of the win was rewarding in many ways. Clay County became the first mountain team to win the championship game in thirty-one years. Besides winning the game and being named the most valuable player, I became the 15th recipient of the Ted Sanford Award. This award is given annually to the player who exemplifies basketball, sportsmanship, citizenship, and academics. My first grade teacher, Mrs. Abner, was on hand to see the award ceremony.

"I was more proud of the academic award he won at the state championship than the awards in sports. Richie was the only player in the history of the Kentucky State Tournament to ever receive both awards in the same year. I think it takes intelligence to play the sport. Most athletes have the ability to excel in their academics; they just don't have the same drive or determination to do as well in class as they do on the court. They have to be disciplined."

"Richie is really special. He was always so disciplined and respectful. It has allowed him to be successful in whatever he's chosen to do. I was glad to have Richie in class. We sure are proud of him. He's done a lot for Clay County, that's for certain."

That game had more meaning to me than just winning the State Championship. The entire team and I had promised to win the whole thing for a friend of ours a year earlier. A cheerleader named Emily Hensley had been with us through every game in the past two years. We were on a road trip to Northern Kentucky where we played in the Famous Recipe Classic. She happened to be my best friend, and we would always eat together after the games. The last night of the tournament the whole group of us gathered in her room to watch a movie. I noticed she wasn't participating. She just sat off to the side by herself. That was not like Emily at all. I knew she

41

had complained of a sore throat before we left for the tournament, but I just thought it was from cheering too much.

The next morning we left for home. By this time, her twin sister had to help her get dressed. One of the parents gave her some tylenol for her fever, and I made a bed for her on the bus out of pillows and blankets. We stopped to

Emily (Em) Hensley

eat, and I brought her some food back, but she couldn't eat. Now she had a very high temperature. We gave her some more tylenol, put cold cloths on her head and waited for the fever to break. It never did. We all knew something was very wrong. She wore a white sweat suit, and her color was just as white as the material. Her family was waiting when we arrived and rushed her to the hospital. She was eventually flown to a hospital in Lexington. Emily died late that night of acute meningitis. I was devastated. Her twin sister and family were destroyed. Her peers lost a wonderful friend. The school lost an excellent cheerleader. I lost my best friend January 10, 1986.

It was dreadful. As a team, we vowed to make it to the finals and win the championship for Emily. I know she helped cheer us on the whole way and even celebrated the victory with us, too.

The victory included an unbelievable "welcome home" by the entire county. As we returned from the state tournament as champions, we were greeted with a caravan on both sides of the Daniel Boone Parkway for about ten miles. We then got on a fire truck that paraded us through town to the high school. Next, we had a rally at school, but the gym couldn't hold even a fourth of the

A Family Affair

crowd. It was an unforgettable feeling, having all that support and pride from so many people. They came from all over the state to help us celebrate.

A Grand Welcome Home for the State Champs

Seeing What Santa Brought

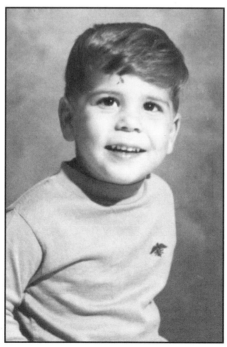

An Early Portrait

Road Game

Batter Up!

Hacker Elementary – County Champs

Richie

One day I went fishing

One day I went fishing.
When I got there I dug up
some worms. I put it on my
hook. I threw it in the water
I geuss I set there an hour.
Then I got a big catfish. Then
I got a bucket of water,
Well I got it and put it
in the water. Then I went
home and set it down. Then
I got the fish and put it in
the fish tank that Rhonda
had. by the time Rhonda
went out the door and come
back in. That catfish had
ate every fish in that tank.
Rhonda screamed and passed
out,

The End.
By Richie

Fish Story – written by six-year-old Richie to sister Rhonda

And They Said He Couldn't Jump

Firing Up the Fans

The Farmer Family – Russ, Mom, Richie, Dad, and Rhonda

Richie at the Charity Stripe

Warm-up Before a Tiger Home Game

Running the Show

Cutting Down the Net After a Regional Title Game

Rambo Richie

Young Guns Two, and Dad

A Post-Game Hug For Mom

A Blue-White Game

Triple-Threat

Richie with Granny Baker

Don't Even Think About It

Richie, For Three

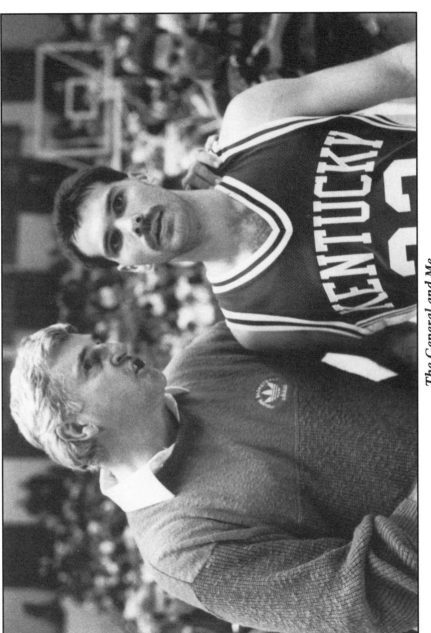

The General and Me

The Impossible Dream – Fulfilled

6

The Key To Success

After the championship, the team and I started speaking in area schools. So many kids don't have anyone to push them, no one to encourage them to stay in school. I personally feel that education is really important. A great number of people graduating from college have a hard time finding a job, so it's even more difficult for those without a high school diploma. I believe an education helps a person communicate and understand people better. It allows them to know what's going on around them. Kids can motivate themselves to do anything they want to do. They just need the nudging and support from their parents. They need to realize how important an education can be to them.

We encouraged the kids to stay in school, and thought the message would come easier from people they looked up to. After the championship was a perfect time to speak to them. They were proud of us, and many boys and girls wanted a part of our victory. This was one way they could have it: to identify with us. We knew many of the kids, which helped us to understand their situations. That made it easier to get through to them. They responded well to our talks.

My senior year in high school I started working for Forward in the Fifth. Orville "Dobber" Smith started the division called "Friends of Education." They give scholarships to children in order for them to further their education. They started by giving autographed pictures of me to all the kids in grade school. I went around and spoke to all the students encouraging them to stay in school. It was amazing what an effect it had on the smaller children. I've had kids come up to me and my family, or they call and say, **"You tell Richie I'm gonna stay in school."** If I helped one student, it was well worth the time and effort.

School has always been important to me. I would come home from high school, finish my homework and then go play ball. I made it a habit. I worked hard to make good grades when I could have done half the work and made average grades, but I'd have known I didn't do my best. Making good grades gives you a sense of accomplishment. Knowing you did your best is good for your self-esteem. If you set your mind to something, I believe you can accomplish whatever it is, or at least get pretty close. Working hard in school isn't always fun, but when you succeed, it gives you a good feeling deep down inside just to know you did it. Even when I bombed out on a test or something, I didn't sit back and say, "That's it. I can't do it." I took the attitude that it may have gotten me this time, but I'd get it next time. Then I'd do better.

That's all you can do. That's the reason I spoke in schools. I wanted people to begin to believe they should always do their best no matter what they were doing. I wanted to encourage the students about their decision to stay in school. It's easy to quit. That's just not the way I think. One of my greatest fears is that I will look back on my life and think I could have done better, and then not have the chance to do it over. I want to know I did my best at everything, in school as well as in sports. I was valedictorian of my eighth grade class. I graduated sixth in a class of 200 in high school, and I held one of our class offices each year. I set goals for myself and worked toward them.

7

"To Whom Much Is Given, Much Will Be Required"

My family is, without a doubt, the most important thing in my life. As far back as I can remember, they have been supportive of everything I did. In addition to basketball, Russ and I also played baseball throughout high school, and we played football for a while. When Russ and I had games on the same day, one parent would be at my game and the other would be at Russ's. My sister Rhonda also loved watching us play, and she rarely missed a game. I don't know how our parents stood such a hectic schedule.

Basketball Brothers

One of the great things about Russ and me is that we were never jealous of each other. You know, Russ is a great ball player. If he had played for any other team, he would have been the superstar. Some people tell us that Russ couldn't get enough publicity because of me. That was hard for us to accept. In his senior year, however, Russ finally got the recognition he deserved. He was great, and his team had a terrific season. People always said he played in my shadow, but without Russ and the other guys on the team, we couldn't have won the state title.

A Proud Dad

When we hang out together and people see us, they always say, "That's Richie's brother," and I hate that for him. I'm sure there were times when he thought, "Gee, I can never do anything as Russ, I'm always Richie's brother," but we were always happy for what the other one did. I don't think we were ever jealous of each other at all. Russ had his own recognition in both basketball and especially baseball. I really love Russ for the way he handled it.

Not only were my parents and siblings faithful followers, but my uncles, aunts, and grandparents were as well. They tried to see whatever games they could and always listened to the radio if unable to attend. Each family member and friend share in the history of who I am and where I've been. That's what it's all about, the pride that comes from loving and supporting your family. Some of my family are real characters.

My great grand-father, Logan Baker, was the minister of the Big Creek Church of Christ. We attended the church from the time I was a child until I graduated from high school. He was a good pastor, and loved to watch Russ and me play ball.

On one occasion, when he was ninety-one years old, Poppy (our nickname for him) was very sick.

Poppy Baker

The family rushed him to the hospital. The doctor wanted to put him in the Intensive Care Unit because of his severely low blood pressure.

When the nurse told him he was to go to ICU, he said, **"I don't want to miss Richie and Russ play ball tonight."** The nurse arranged for a radio to be in his room. By the time the game started, his blood pressure had returned to normal.

68

After that they moved him to a private room. He listened to the game through some headphones. The nurses raised his bed up, and then made many trips back and forth, checking on him and the game.

It was hard to stop smiling when you looked at that little old man with a head full of snow-white hair. His face glowed as he listened to every play of our game.

Poppy Baker not only had a great sense of humor, he also was a great storyteller. He would gather the grandchildren around him and tell hunting tales, ghost stories, and boyhood yarns for hours at a time. Nobody ever thought to ask if the stories were true. Who cared?

He married couples by the hundreds, and baptized probably two or three thousand people during his fifty-five years as a minister. My great-grandmother, Addie Marcum Baker, died before I could know her. He said she was a loving wife and mother. I know he has been a tremendous influence on my religious faith.

Besides my great-grandfather, my grandparents: Granny Wolfe, Papoo, Granny Baker, and Papaw Farmer, along with my uncles: Kenneth F., Russell, Michael, Jackie, Charles, and Kenneth B., and my aunts: Karen and Linda, have all supported and in some special way influenced me.

Our family was active in church, and I learned the Bible stories at an early age. Most people never ask about your spiritual beliefs, and I doubt if many people thought much about mine, but I not only know my Bible, I believe it.

When I was in high school, I was in a group called Soldiers for Christ. The group went to different churches to sing, give testimonies and lead the service for an hour. There weren't many calls for me to sing solos, thank goodness, and sometimes we would be nervous around the kids we didn't know. We still had a great time, and I

69

enjoyed doing it.

I think about how difficult it is when people don't always do the right things. Someone sees you out doing something you shouldn't be doing and they have to think you are the biggest hypocrite in the world. That bothers me, because so many people recognize me now, and I know I'm not perfect. I make mistakes just like everyone else. I don't always do things the way some people think I should, but I try to do my best. I believe when we are trying our best, that is what pleases God.

If I have a favorite verse of scripture, it's not because I get inspiration from it, but because it makes me feel a little uneasy and personally challenged. The verse is in the book of Luke, 12:33, and says, "To whom much is given, much will be required." I know in some ways God has given me very much. A good home, wonderful parents and friends, a good mind and certain talents. It is scary for me to think about what exactly He will require from me. I want to touch as many lives as I can, especially now that I have the opportunity.

8

Coaches' Thoughts

My senior year of school amazed me. In basketball, at least, our team had drawn enough attention to our playing ability that all eyes were on Clay County. We were the first mountain team to win the championship in 31 years. We were ranked number one in the state with no player over 6'1". We got to go back to the state tournament that year, 1988, and play Ballard again in the final game.

"That game never really came down to a last second shot," says Coach Keith. "Richie came out and he was hot. He kept us in the game the first half. At one stretch in the second half, he missed three or four shots in a row. Then he started making plays to get everybody else shots, to get everybody else open, but the entire team was exhausted. You could see it in their faces; their legs just weren't there. Everybody was missing shots. They were all so

The Agony of Defeat

71

tired. We were about two steps behind Ballard the whole way. I realized somebody had to get us back in the game. I knew Richie realized it, too. He could tell we all were looking to him to do it. Richie knew he had to score."

"I remembered Richie telling Doug Flynn before the game that he didn't know how he would get through the game because he couldn't feel his legs. The team had taken a beating just six hours before from Pleasure Ridge Park. It had been such a physical game and somehow ended in our favor 92-90."

'88 State Tourney MVP

"Even though he was exhausted, Richie said afterward, 'I reached deep within myself and found the strength to push even harder. I wasn't going to just quit. We had worked too hard.' I knew this championship would not go into overtime this year. Although Richie scored an incredible 51 points that game, we lost 88-79."

"That game showed everybody that Richie could play

for any school. It was the breaking point for a lot of things," said Richard and Virginia. "It proved the great ability he had and the great number of fans he had attracted throughout his high school career."

A proud Clay County coach, Bobby Keith said, "Richie Farmer was one of the best high school basketball players that ever played the game. Nobody in the nation, game after game, for what he did for his team, ever stacked up to what Richie did in high school. He outplayed one All-American after another consistently."

"One game during his senior year, we were playing a small school that wasn't good at all that year. Jackson hadn't been hitting. Russ and Chadwell hadn't scored many points. It had been pretty much all Richie for the last three games, and I told Richie, 'Tonight, I don't want you to worry about scoring. I want you to get Jackson 27, Russ and Chad about 25 each, and get Boxhead some points. That night I think he had 27 assists. Jackson scored 29, Russ had 22, Chadwell had 24, and Rich had

Charlie Robinson, Kevin Jackson, Eugene "Boxhead" Rawlings, Russ Farmer, Russ Chadwell, and Richie

73

15. I didn't want to tell the team what had happened, but I went over to Richie and told him I thought that was the best game he'd played all year. That's the type of player he was. He did what he had to do to win and keep his teammates happy."

Coach Keith went on to say, "Well, I've always said that I've had players who could jump better, run faster and some that probably could shoot better; in fact, his brother Russ could probably shoot better. The one thing that Richie had that I've never found in any other of my high school players is mental maturity. From the time he was in the eighth grade he could take a team and play with the type of coolness and character that you just don't find in teenagers. The only thing I can compare it to is Olympic athletes. You see these thirteen year olds that go out to compete, knowing it's being televised all over the world, and they put on a gold medal performance. It's just amazing. I can't imagine a thirteen year old performing under those conditions."

"Richie was that type of athlete," Keith attests. "The bigger the ballgame, the better he played. The more pressure you put on him, the better he responded. I think only special people can do that — exceptional athletes. Richie is one of those athletes. I would put him up against anybody in the nation. You give me Richie running my team, and I'll beat anybody in the country."

Another well-respected coach from Mason County High School, Allen Feldhaus, said, "If I had to pick five players in the nation, in a pinch, I'd want Richie among the five. He has to be one of the greatest pressure players I've ever seen."

After high school, Richie had many schools try to recruit him. One such school was Kentucky Weslyan. Its head coach, Wayne Chapman, said, "There's a lot of players that can jump higher, and run quicker... but he's a winner. He plays the game the way it should be played."

Dale Brown said, "Richie's one of the two best guards in the nation." He was also speaking of Chris Jackson. After Richie signed with UK and Chris had signed with LSU, Coach Brown said on ESPN, "I recruited two guards last year. I recruited the two best guards in the nation: one of them I got, one of them I didn't."

Blowing By Jackson

9

From A Tiger To A Wildcat

After my senior year in high school, my dream, literally, came true. The Wildcats offered me my own uniform. As excited as I was to play basketball for Kentucky, leaving Manchester wasn't easy. I knew I would miss my family and friends. What I didn't know was how much they would miss me.

I heard my sister Rhonda say that the day I left town was the hardest day in her life. She said Mom and Dad had a hard time, too. It was a big change for all of us. They looked to me as the peace-keeper in the family since I could always talk with anyone. I found out that keeping the peace at home was a whole lot different from keeping it at the University.

I will say my freshman year was rough. It's hard for all the new students to adjust to different rules, food, classes, and thousands of strangers. Remember, there were almost as many kids in my classes as there were people in Manchester. I think the toughest adjustment was to go from being a team leader to being a team player. I knew that several great players from Eastern Kentucky had quit, and I was determined more than ever to stay. In the toughest, most disappointing days, I believe my family's support and my early Christian training got me through.

I learned that finding a letter from home was one of

the most important events of my day. I was in an unfamiliar position, and calling home was about the only thing I felt I could do.

U.K. Freshman

When I first came to UK, I didn't know what to expect. Our first game day we had to wear a coat and tie. I didn't even own one. My parents had to bring one to me that day.

Everyone has times when they are really low. I went through some of those times at UK. I will admit that for a while I wanted to quit and go back to the mountains. I felt fortunate to have a few good friends from home in Lexington. Some of those friends are Jim and Judy Rose. Jim and Judy always try to help a mountain boy (especially from Clay County) if he is willing to give his best. Whenever I felt like quitting, one of my friends from home would encourage me. One such friend is Bill Ed Mobley, whom I have known all my life. For the last five years, though, we've been like brothers. He's one of those friends that I can kid with, and neither one of us will get mad.

He used to tell me, **"Many people say you will never make it at Kentucky. They don't think you are tall enough, strong enough or fast enough, but,"** he said, "both you and I know better."

He reminded me time and time again that even though practices were rough, I could make it. Most of all, he told me I was representing all the other players in Eastern Kentucky who were playing on dirt courts and dreaming of wearing Kentucky blue. Two other special friends are Ted and Debbie Cook. Ted and Debbie have always been there for me.

One of the encouraging bright spots my freshman year was the Ole Miss game on Senior Night, when I hit the game winner. Mr. Cawood Ledford expressed that game best as he called it in those final moments.

The Winning Shot

"The ball comes into Farmer... Farmer goes across the time line... he may take it himself...he dribbles down the right side... throws into Ellis...Ellis kicks it back out to Farmer...Farmer goes up for threeee, GOT IT! Kentucky wins!"

That was a great win on which to end such a difficult year. It had been difficult not only because of the physical stress we endured, but also because of the NCAA investigation. Probation would follow. Our final record was 13-19.

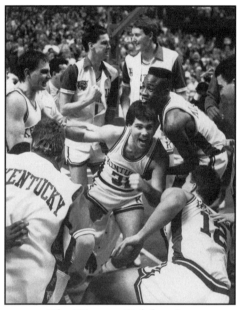

The Victory Celebration

The probation period started my sophomore year. The team could have no live broadcast games, no post-season play, and could not participate in tournaments. Of course, these were just a few of the sanctions placed on the University that year. Once the 1988-89 year was over, many UK players chose to play for other schools. With Coach Sutton gone, along with many of the staff, the newly hired athletics director, C.M. Newton, gathered the remaining eight players together to talk about who the new coach would be. He said, **"I'm going to get you** guys the best coach that UK can get. We're not going to rush things. I thought we would have had a coach by now, but we want to make sure we get who we want. We're not going to be in any rush. If we don't find a coach, I'll coach you guys myself."

Playing for UK had been a dream. I had at least gotten that far. All of us on the team that year could have gone to play somewhere else. At that time there was Reggie Hanson, Deron Felhaus, John Pelphrey, Sean Woods, and myself, all of whom had roots in Kentucky. We stayed. Derrick Miller and Jonathon Davis also stayed, while the other guys left. We made a commitment that we wanted to help Kentucky basketball get back to what we had always known it to be, because Kentucky basketball meant something. It was special even with all the sanctions. When we put Kentucky across our chests, we went out on the floor to win. We were willing to do whatever it took to see that it happened. As individuals, I think we each made the commitment, and as a team, we understood that commitment. We just couldn't leave the program in the shape it was in. UK had been our dream, our only logical choice. We were not going to turn our backs on what we had worked so hard to achieve.

Coach Newton was not joking when he said he'd get the best. The team welcomed Rick Pitino to the Bluegrass for the beginning of the 1989-90 season. The first time I spoke to Coach Pitino was over the phone. He called to tell me things he expected, and wanted to get to know me. Then, when he got down here, we were all kidding around and he said, "I talked to Richie for twelve minutes on the phone. I understood about two minutes of the conversation."

I told him, "You did much better than I did. I only understood about thirty seconds of what you said."

From then on we had a running joke about understanding each other's accents. Even the press picked up on it. Rarely a presentation went by that someone didn't mention it.

Coach Pitino expected 110%. He has a tremendous work ethic; he's probably one of the hardest working coaches in America. He's very focused.

Richie and Coach Pitino

As a sophomore, he called me into his office. He said that in order for me to play at this level, I had to drop twenty-five pounds, get quicker, get stronger, and change my entire set of habits. I told him I'd do anything to get some time on the playing floor. I knew I was a ballplayer. I knew I could do the job. I walked out of his office motivated to do it. I felt he was being honest with me. Everything he does he does for a purpose. He has a plan. Two of his greatest assets are his work ethic and his motivational skills. I was encouraged, and thought that

81

if I made the necessary changes, I would be playing. I have to admit, I was kind of overwhelmed at first. I had to change my eating habits, routine, everything. I lost twenty-five pounds in two months. My body fat that year went from fifteen or sixteen percent to eight percent. In my senior year, it was about six percent. He stayed on me the whole time.

The New Richie

I knew going into any collegiate sport the physical end of it was going to be very strenuous. You just accept it. To be honest, there were a few times when the mental side was much more difficult. The tough part is if the practice drills become personal, and you are singled out for reasons you don't understand. It wears you down to take more discouragement than encouragement.

There were times when the team ran laps until I thought our legs would fall off. When all the guys were running and you could see the pain on their faces, it gave me extra incentive not to quit. Other times, when I had to run alone — that's when the doubts crept in.

The fans only see the games. I don't think they can really appreciate how hard a Kentucky team practices. Many times we started practicing at 5:30 a.m. That was just the beginning of our day. We had classes and labs, along with more practices, and maybe even a game.

Another person very instrumental in helping me lose the weight was Ray 'Rock' Oliver. He was the strength coach, and in my opinion, the best strength coach in the nation. There were times when we had our differences, but we became the closest of friends. It's a friendship that will last a lifetime.

I played one of my best games my sophmore year against LSU. Their team was a force to be reckoned with because it included great players like Shaquille O'Neal, Stanley Roberts, and Chris Jackson. Dale Brown had his players foul me on purpose to put me on the line. I made six of six free throws down the stretch, and we won 100-95.

The worst game we played that year was at Kansas. We lost by fifty-five points (150-95). It was the worst beating I ever had, probably the worst beating any of us ever had.

We approached every game during probation as if it were our NCAA tournament. We were expected to lose each year we were on probation, but that didn't happen. We ended up with a 14-14 won/lost record that year.

We looked forward to playing Kansas the next year in Rupp Arena. We counted down the days until that game. It wasn't only the players, but the fans, University, and media that looked forward to that rematch. It seemed as if the entire Commonwealth supported us. This time we won by seventeen points. There was a great deal of pride on the line that game. It was a big win for the team and a turning point for Kentucky basketball.

That year we had the best record in the Southeastern Conference (SEC); we knew we were back on top. Our won/lost record was 22-6.

Because we could not play in any tournaments my junior year, the Senior Night game was our last for that season. It was after that game that Coach Pitino announced that the upcoming four seniors would be co-captains of the team.

10

My Senior Year

My senior year was extremely meaningful to me. We had a won/lost record of 29-7. One of the outstanding games my senior year was the Notre Dame game. In that game, I scored twenty-two points in the first half.

I also played a part in our win against Mississippi State.

"When Richie made eight of eight free throws at the end of the Mississippi State game this year...," Coach Rick Pitino said, "Thank God for Richie Farmer on the foul line. If I had somebody shooting free throws, or shooting key shots, for that situation, I'd rather have Richie than anybody else."

We finally had a chance to play in the tournaments, and I would do my part to try and make our team number one again. The first tournament we were eligible for was the SEC in Birmingham. We defeated Vanderbilt, LSU, and Alabama to become SEC Tournament Champions.

We almost pulled off the impossible. We became one of the Elite Eight in the NCAA Tournament. We beat Old Dominion, Iowa State, and the University of Massachusetts, before finally losing to Duke. It was an incredible season, and one we could all be proud of.

The pressure from ballgames is not the only thing a Wildcat must handle. Playing ball for the University of

Kentucky carries as much pressure from the time demand standpoint as well. I don't want to sound like I regretted a minute of it. There were a lot of people tugging at me and making requests to do this or that. Some of the time, they just didn't understand that we players had a life just like theirs. You know, sometimes all you want is to be alone.

One of the things that goes with being a Wildcat is autographs. It's something I always love to do. After all, it's special when people want something signed with your name on it. You wouldn't believe when I've been asked for my autograph. I could be out to eat with my family or my girlfriend. I could be on the golf course or at a high school game, even in restrooms and doctors' offices. It can be funny in a kind of disturbing way. I hope they ask me for mine the rest of my life, but I wouldn't mind if they could pick better times and places. Anyway, I try to never say 'no,' especially to the kids.

The Four Seniors with UK Great Larry Conley

No player can do everything the fans expect. It's hard to wave and try to remember all the names. Even when you try not to hurt anyone's feelings, you just simply can't sign enough autographs.

With everything the four of us seniors had been through, we never even dreamed about how very special our Senior year would be. An awards ceremony is given each year at the end of the season. In the past, after the individual awards were presented, they usually gave a Senior award. I began to wonder what was going on when they failed to announce this special award. C.M. Newton went to the center line and asked all the seniors and their families to come join him. That's when he started talking about all that we had done for the University and what our staying had meant to them. He then asked us to turn and look up to the rafters of Rupp Arena. I had no idea what was happening. As I turned and looked, there it was – my number 32. It was the biggest shock of my whole life. I could remember all the days we would go to Rupp and practice, lying on the floor stretching, looking up at those retired jerseys. At times I'd even make comments to some of the guys. "Gosh, look up there at all the great players and legends. Wouldn't it be great to have our jerseys hanging up there some day?" Then I'd think back on all I had accomplished personally, and I knew I would never be there. As a boy growing up, I dreamed of playing for UK, and of having some great games. I never dared dream of having my jersey hanging up there with all the legends that played for Kentucky. I never, ever dreamed of that. Having my jersey hang among the rafters right next to Coach Rupp is so special to me. It's made everything I've gone through worth it.

We had an extremely hectic schedule during the barnstorming tour. The tour was designed for the seniors to travel the state in order to meet and play in front of

Kentucky fans. We played local teams all over the state. I think we played twenty-four games this spring. During the barn-storming tour, we were going to class full-time and playing six games a week. We would leave from class, get our bags, drive two and a half hours, eat on the way, go in the gym and sign autographs for an hour. Then we'd go right back in, change, stretch, warm-up, play, and sign autographs afterwards. You have to have a time limit for signing, or you'd be there all night. We appreciate everybody loving us and wanting our autographs, but there's no way we could sign every one of them.

The most emotional game for me during that tour was when we played in Clay County. It was great to play in front of my hometown as an official Wildcat. Not everyone had been able to see me play in person as a Wildcat, which is why I enjoyed the 110 points I scored during that game.

Richie Immortalized with Coach Rupp

11

Parting Shots

I'm just twenty-three years old, my life is only beginning, and yet I feel a great amount of pressure to not let anyone down.

A while ago, when we had an autograph session, a lady came up to me and said, "My grandson and I just wanted you to know that he thinks he's you, Richie. He walks around calling himself Richie. He tries to dress like Richie and even talks like Richie."

You know I've heard that a lot, and I like to speak to as many kids as I can. I guess if I sat and thought about it, it would be hard to think of myself as someone's hero. When you have kids and everyone looking up to you like this, you want to do everything right. You never want to make a mistake.

One of the great qualities Richie has is to make others feel important. It certainly is a quality that deserves notice. While at UK, Richie continued to work in the community. He made a point to help others. Jennifer Garda, a nurse, offered her story about Richie.

"Valentine's Day this year was during the Veteran's Appreciation Week. Rick Pitino, Junior Braddy, and Richie Farmer came to the floor to see all the patients where I had nurse's duty every day. One patient had a cancer of his nose and had it removed, along with part of his lips and skin underneath his eye. He also had a tracheotomy. Hardly anybody could understand him. Even the staff that had been working with him daily had difficulty. It was frustrating for him to communicate. Richie went in to see him with Rick and Junior. The patient didn't know who anyone was except Richie. They talked about how many points he scored in some games, and Richie understood every word that this man said. Richie had no problems. He held his hand and looked him straight in the eye. He made him feel special. It really meant a lot to that patient to see him. I thought it was wonderful how Richie related to that man. Now the patient is fine. He had been a recluse of sorts, hardly ever leaving his room. But after that visit, he started getting out. It really did a lot for that guy's self-esteem."

"He saw all the patients. They all wanted autographs. They loved him, and he was great. He talked to everybody. Many of the patients were from Eastern Kentucky. They all followed the UK games. I never thought about basketball players being regular people before that night. I'll never forget how wonderful Richie was to all those patients."

I suppose my life in the future will not be so different from these first years. I've always tried to work hard, and live a full, happy, and successful life. What I mean by being successful has something to do with reaching goals and earning a living. I think money is necessary, but it's not everything. Having a lot of money would be great, but I don't know if it would necessarily make me happy. Being happy is one of the most important things in life besides family. If you have billions of dollars and you're not happy, you have nothing.

I know many people who don't have much money at all, but I know they're happy; that's what counts. I also would like to have a family because I love kids.

I love to spend time with my nephew, Daniel. He is such a free spirit at three and a half. Any time I go to Manchester, I stop at his house and pick him up before I do anything else. I like watching him experience new things. This spring, my parents brought Daniel to Rupp Arena several hours before a game. I carried him out on the floor and let him shoot baskets. I was holding him up, and he was making baskets in Rupp Arena at three and a half; then he met Cawood Ledford! I couldn't believe he was doing this at his age; it took me nineteen years to do all that. He means the world to me. I couldn't do without the time we spend together. He's my best pal.

Richie, with his Nephew and Best Pal, Daniel

I know one thing for certain: all that I've learned through basketball will help me achieve whatever I set my sights on. I know I do my best when someone challenges me. I believe I learned that from basketball. If everything's going smooth I think something must be wrong. It's better for me to have certain goals and know I will have to work hard to achieve them. I like to prove myself to myself every day.

My training has inspired me to set certain goals in life. If the goals aren't high enough, I feel like it's up to me to raise them. I don't know why, but there is this fire in me to do things that are difficult. I believe the business world respects someone who isn't afraid of hard work.

"Richie likes to play hard as well," says golfing buddy Bill Ed Mobley.

"When we go golfing, we usually bet a Pepsi as we enter the turn, since we'll be getting a drink anyway. Richie might be playing pitiful, but as soon as I pressure him with the bet...BAM, that's all he needs. Something in him kicks in. His athletic skills and competitiveness go into overdrive. He'll suddenly make every drive and every putt to beat me. Richie's got that as much or more than anyone. He can't settle for less. It's innate in him. Richie will succeed no matter what he does."

I hope what's ahead will be even better than all I've done so far. In some ways I try not to think about the future, but I know in my heart I've got to operate by a new game plan.

First of all, I've got to face the fact that my life without basketball will be different. You know, family, school and hoops is all I've ever done. Now that I'm getting opportunities, the main thing is to figure out what's best for me and what I would like the most, and then make the right decision.

Secondly, I am trying to make sure the people who are

making me offers are upstanding and honest. When I played basketball and we lost a game or two, there was always next season, but the decisions I'm making now are for life. I'm trying to be careful.

Finally, I am going to do some things that Richie Farmer wants to do, like fishing, hunting or traveling. Maybe if I want to go to Florida and stay a week I can do it. I don't have to call anybody and ask them. I don't have to check and make sure it's not breaking some rule. Now, I can wake up and say, "I think I'll play some golf today," and I can actually head for the golf course. It is the first time I haven't had "next season" to work toward.

Whatever happens the rest of my life, I intend to do my best. I've always played to win. When you lose, it hurts. In fact, I know you can't always win, but when you lose, it seems to hurt deep down inside. That's what keeps the whole picture of life in focus for me – I just can't see losing.

You have to be a good loser. You can't live your life blaming your weaknesses and mistakes on others. You don't have to like it, and you can work your tail off to see it never happens again.

I can't do anything about losing to Duke in that terrific NCAA game. The shot went in, and I went home. But I'll promise you one thing: myself, the three other seniors, and all the other Wildcats will be back in Rupp next season. Some will be in the stands, and others in the game. To every last one of you, we'll give the best we can to continue the tradition of the Kentucky Wildcats.

Before every Clay County High School game, all the players would gather in front of our bench and put our heads together. We did it to symbolize our togetherness. I know that's what makes Kentucky basketball so special. Whether you watch Kentucky basketball on television, or listen to a game on the radio, or sit in the arena, your heads are touching Kentucky fans all over this country. And that's what makes winners of us all.

Togetherness

A special thanks to Doug Reece without whose idea and encouragement there would have been no book, and to John Lang for his legal advice and commitment to this project.

FOR ADDITIONAL COPIES OF

RICHIE

Write: **Antex Corporation**
120 Dennis Drive
Lexington, KY 40503
(606) 276-3896

Send me _____ copies at $9.95 per copy plus shipping charge of $3.00 per copy.

Send me _____ Blue-letter Edition copies at $14.95 per copy plus shpping charge of $3.00 per copy.

Name: _____

Address: _____

City: _____ State _____ Zip _____

Total Enclosed _____

Make check or money order payable to Antex Corporation.

- -

FOR ADDITIONAL COPIES OF

RICHIE

Write: **Antex Corporation**
120 Dennis Drive
Lexington, KY 40503
(606) 276-3896

Send me _____ copies at $9.95 per copy plus shipping charge of $3.00 per copy.

Send me _____ Blue-letter Edition copies at $14.95 per copy plus shpping charge of $3.00 per copy.

Name: _____

Address: _____

City: _____ State _____ Zip _____

Total Enclosed _____

Make check or money order payable to Antex Corporation.

- -

FOR ADDITIONAL COPIES OF

RICHIE

Write: **Antex Corporation**
120 Dennis Drive
Lexington, KY 40503
(606) 276-3896

Send me _____ copies at $9.95 per copy plus shipping charge of $3.00 per copy.

Send me _____ Blue-letter Edition copies at $14.95 per copy plus shpping charge of $3.00 per copy.

Name: _____

Address: _____

City: _____ State _____ Zip _____

Total Enclosed _____

Make check or money order payable to Antex Corporation.

Other Publications from ANTEX

First Love: A Story About Basketball – *A basketball player's reflections on growing up in Kentucky playing basketball.*

Wee-Dolph, the Tiniest Reindeer – *A lovable children's book with beautiful color pictures telling the story of the tiniest reindeer of all.*

These and other fine publications available
at your local bookstore, or from

Antex Corporation
120 Dennis Drive
Lexington, KY 40503
(606) 276-3896